The U.S. Army in World War II

PETER BENOIT

Children's Press®
An Imprint of Scholastic Inc.
New York Toronto London Auckland Sydney
Mexico City New Delhi Hong Kong
Danbury, Connecticut

Content Consultant

James Marten, PhD
Professor and Chair, History Department
Marquette University, Milwaukee, Wisconsin

Library of Congress Cataloging-in-Publication Data
Benoit, Peter, 1955–
The U.S. Army in World War II / by Peter Benoit.
  pages cm. — (A true book)
Includes bibliographical references and index.
ISBN 978-0-531-20496-2 (library binding) — ISBN 978-0-531-21731-3 (paperback)
1. United States. Army—History—World War, 1939–1945—Juvenile literature. 2. Soldiers—United
States—History—20th century—Juvenile literature. 3. World War, 1939–1945—United States—
Juvenile literature. I. Title.
 D769.B43 2014
 940.54'1273—dc23   2014003935

Front cover: U.S. infantry troops with tank
Back cover: U.S. mortar squad firing on German troops near the Rhine River

Find the Truth!

Everything you are about to read is true *except* for one of the sentences on this page.

Which one is **TRUE**?

T or F   Some women fought in combat units for the U.S. Army during World War II.

T or F   Civilian groups in Germany worked to overthrow the country's Nazi government.

Find the answers in this book.

3

Contents

THE **BIG** TRUTH!

**American tank troops practice
just before the country
entered World War II.**

EMERGENCY RATION D

To be eaten slowly (in about a half hour). Can be dissolved by crumbling into a cup of boiling water if desired as a beverage.

INGREDIENTS:

Chocolate, Sugar, Skim Milk Powder, Cocoa Fat, Oat Flour, Artificial Flavoring, 0.45 mg. Vitamin B₁ (Thiamin Hydrochloride).

4 OUNCES NET - 600 CALORIES

The army supplied troops with emergency rations.

More than 150,000 women volunteered for the Women's Army Corps.

German soldiers display
the national flag of Nazi
Germany during a parade.

CHAPTER 1

Gearing Up

World War II began in Europe when Germany invaded Poland in September 1939. German **Nazi** leader Adolf Hitler wanted to establish a new German empire across Europe. Within the year, Germany also invaded Holland, Belgium, France, and Norway. In July 1940, Germany began attacking Britain.

To the east, Japan invaded Manchuria in 1931 and had plans to take over China, Southeast Asia, and the Pacific. In 1940, Japan officially joined forces with Germany and Italy. The three became known as the Axis powers.

← Symbols used by the Nazi Party are illegal in Germany today.

The Army of the United States

As fighting worsened overseas, Americans decided to strengthen their army. They wanted to be prepared in case the United States was attacked. The U.S. government began to **draft** young men in 1940. The country entered the war alongside Great Britain as part of the Allied powers in 1941. Before the war ended in 1945, the United States had drafted about 10 million men. People also volunteered. More than 6 million people voluntarily enlisted between 1941 and 1945.

About 60 percent of the men in the U.S. military during World War II had been drafted.

A woman constructs ammunition at a factory.

The army did not just need soldiers. It also needed equipment. The U.S. military put people to work making tanks, planes, guns, and **ammunition**. Food was needed to feed the army and the people on the home front. Therefore, the U.S. government was careful not to draft all of the nation's farmers. The draft board made sure there were still men left to work on U.S. farms.

U.S. soldiers drive tanks during an exercise.

Army Units

In 1942, the army was organized into three branches: ground forces, air forces, and service forces. Ground forces included troops such as the infantry, who fought on foot. Some ground forces drove tanks or dropped out of airplanes. The Army Air Force included pilots and their crew. Some air force members specialized in fighter planes. Others worked with bomber or transport planes.

Service forces included doctors, engineers, and other workers who provided services to troops. The medical **corps** helped wounded men on the battlefield. Engineers helped clear trees and brush and maintain roads. They built bridges, ports, and hospitals. The signal corps used radios to communicate over long distances. Service forces were also in charge of transporting troops and keeping the army supplied.

Army engineers create roads on French beaches by laying wire mats on the sand.

Training an Army

New soldiers had to be trained before going to war. Basic training prepared soldiers for the physical challenges of battle and for life in the army. Soldiers spent months exercising to build strength and speed. They learned how to care for and shoot weapons. Drill sergeants taught them how to fight, march, and dress like a soldier. New troops also had to learn how to interact with people above and below them in rank.

Army training included learning how to aim and shoot various weapons.

12

Parachute troops were used for the first time in World War II.

Paratroopers jump out of an airplane above Georgia during training.

In addition, soldiers were trained to do their particular jobs. Some learned to operate tanks. Others trained to jump out of airplanes, work radios, or treat injuries. Pilots learned about air combat. Men with the same job trained with one another for several weeks. Finally, troops were loaded on ships and sent to war.

A U.S. soldier rests in his foxhole, or shelter, in Italy.

CHAPTER 2

You're in the Army

Every army job brought its own challenges. Men on the ground faced rifles, grenades, and land mines. Soldiers in vehicles were the targets of rockets. Cannons or planes shot down air force crewmen.

Soldiers battled nature as well. When it rained, they were covered in mud and filth. When it was hot, some suffered heatstroke. In the Pacific, men caught diseases such as malaria. On winter nights in Europe, some soldiers got frostbite.

← Italy officially surrendered six days before the Allies invaded Italy's mainland.

Soldiers line up for food during the Battle of the Bulge against German troops in Belgium.

Dogfaces

The men in the infantry were sometimes called dogfaces. They wore identification tags called dog tags. The small, portable tents they carried were called pup tents. When they weren't moving, the soldiers dug foxholes for shelter.

Infantrymen's lives were difficult. They marched in snow, rain, or intense heat. Sometimes they could not shower or change clothes for weeks. They often rested back-to-back. This allowed them to see enemy soldiers approaching from any direction.

Of the military groups, members of the infantry faced the greatest danger. Roughly 70 percent of Americans injured or killed in the war were in the army infantry. Infantrymen generally fought on the front lines. This means they faced enemy forces directly. When they weren't fighting, they helped transport food, ammunition, and medicine. They kept their own supplies in pockets, belts, or bags.

Infantrymen wade toward Makin Island in the Pacific during the Battle of Makin.

Tank Divisions

Men in armored tank divisions faced their own dangers. Most of these men fought in the M4 Sherman tank. The tanks offered some protection to the crew inside. However, the protection was not perfect. Certain weapons could rip through a Sherman tank's armor. A direct hit could cause a fire to break out inside the tank, exploding the ammunition inside.

Troops drive a Sherman tank through the streets of Torino di Sangro, Italy.

Army mechanics repair a damaged track on a Sherman tank.

Sherman tanks generally had a crew of five men. A commander led the crew. There was also a driver, a gunner, a person to load ammunition, and someone who helped drive the tank or fire guns. Mechanics were responsible for maintaining tanks and other machinery. They worked to keep tanks in top condition. They also repaired any damages that occurred.

The crewmen of a bomber talk beside their plane.

Air Attack

Serving in the air force was also dangerous. One accurate shot from the ground or from another plane could destroy a fighter or bomber. The stress of combat could be exhausting. Crewmen generally flew dozens of missions before being replaced. To make it through the war, they found ways to stay positive. For example, they often decorated their leather jackets with lucky charms and cartoon characters.

Civilian Soldiers

Not all soldiers who fought during World War II were members of a country's official military. As Germany took over countries across Europe, **civilians** came together to form **resistance** groups. These "soldiers" stole supplies, disrupted communications, helped threatened people hide or escape, and spied on Nazi officials. Sometimes they went into open battle against the Germans. Resistance efforts took place in every Nazi-occupied country. These included Poland, the Soviet Union, Yugoslavia, France, and even Germany.

The World's Armies

Countries all around the globe became involved in World War II. Germany, Italy, and Japan were the major players of the Axis powers. Great Britain, the Soviet Union, China, and the United States played large roles among the Grand Alliance, or Allies. Here is a little information about the other major armies, aside from the U.S. Army, involved in the war.

Pearl
Harbor
HAWAII

UNITED
STATES

PACIFIC
OCEAN

☐ Allied power
☐ Axis power
☐ Neutral country
— Extent of Axis control
November 1942

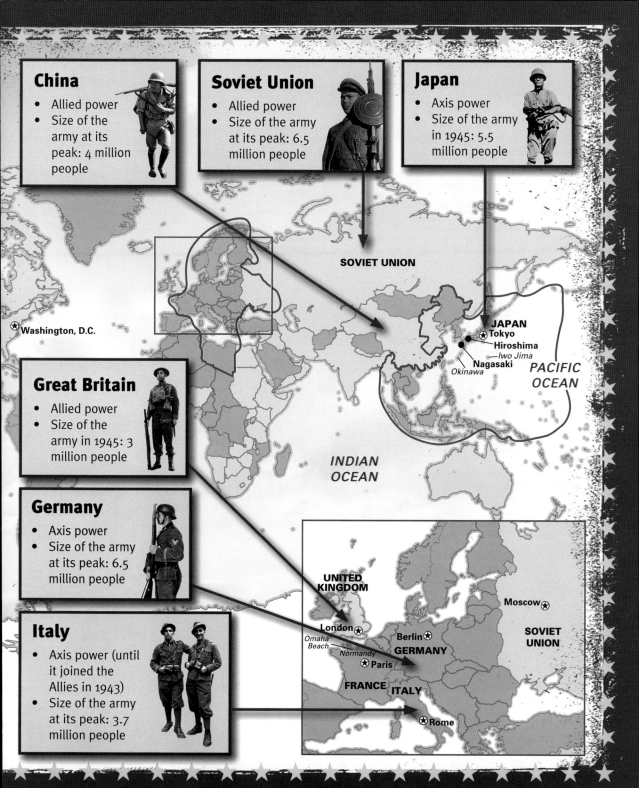

China

- Allied power
- Size of the army at its peak: 4 million people

Soviet Union

- Allied power
- Size of the army at its peak: 6.5 million people

Japan

- Axis power
- Size of the army in 1945: 5.5 million people

Great Britain

- Allied power
- Size of the army in 1945: 3 million people

Germany

- Axis power
- Size of the army at its peak: 6.5 million people

Italy

- Axis power (until it joined the Allies in 1943)
- Size of the army at its peak: 3.7 million people

SOVIET UNION

Washington, D.C.

JAPAN
Tokyo
Hiroshima
Iwo Jima
Nagasaki
Okinawa

PACIFIC OCEAN

INDIAN OCEAN

UNITED KINGDOM

Moscow

London
Omaha Beach
Normandy
Berlin
GERMANY

SOVIET UNION

Paris

FRANCE
ITALY

Rome

A landing craft carries troops, trucks, and supplies to forces in Italy.

CHAPTER 3

Supplies to Survive the War

Keeping the army going was hard work. Soldiers needed food, clothes, shelter, and ammunition. Tanks, planes, and other vehicles required replacement parts and fuel. All these supplies and the troops who used them had to be easy to move. Supplies also had to be made to last.

A quartermaster is in charge of making sure troops are supplied.

Soldiers visit a field kitchen set up in France.

Eating the Alphabet

The army provided different kinds of **rations** in different situations. A rations were the highest quality of food available to troops. They were made of locally grown or frozen foods. Cooks prepared them in field kitchens set up away from the front lines. B rations were also cooked in field kitchens. Unlike A rations, B rations did not need to be refrigerated and would not spoil quickly.

C rations could take the place of B rations. C rations included canned meat dishes and bread. Candy and coffee powders were included in C rations, too. K rations were emergency meals that could fit inside a soldier's pocket. They consisted of hard biscuits, candy, and dry sausages. They were meant to provide meals for only a few days. D rations were another emergency food. They were bitter bars of chocolate that contained oat flour and skim milk powder.

D rations were meant to provide a soldier with a lot of energy without taking up much space among supplies.

The U.S. government purchased almost 118 million D rations in 1942.

EMERGENCY RATION D

To be eaten slowly (in about a half hour). Can be dissolved by crumbling into a cup of boiling water if desired as a beverage.

INGREDIENTS:

Chocolate, Sugar, Skim Milk Powder, Cocoa Fat, Oat Flour, Artificial Flavoring, 0.45 mg. Vitamin B₁ (Thiamin Hydrochloride).

4 OUNCES NET - 600 CALORIES

GI

During the war, the nickname GI for an American soldier became popular. This is most likely connected to the equipment, machines, and other items with which he was surrounded. *GI* first referred to "galvanized iron." Extreme climates caused equipment to rust quickly. Galvanized iron had a protective coating to keep it from rusting. The letters eventually came to mean "government issue." Soldiers began joking that they were government issue war goods.

Nearly everything a soldier carried was issued by the government.

German soldiers sometimes added hidden explosives to everyday objects such as pencils.

Certain soldiers, such as medics, carried extra supplies for their particular job. Medics also had markings, such as a red cross, on their uniforms or helmets to show they were medical workers.

What to Wear

Uniforms were different depending on where soldiers were located. Troops in colder areas wore wool uniforms. In North Africa and tropical areas, they wore lightweight cotton.

Many soldiers carried most of their own supplies. To cut down on a soldier's load, objects often had many uses. For example, a helmet could hold water so a soldier could bathe.

The *V* in V-mail stands for "victory."

Workers inspect and separate a collection of V-mail letters.

Letters from Home

Letters from home helped GIs keep their spirits up. However, mail took up space on airplanes that could be used for supplies instead. The government also worried that enemy spies might read the letters to gain information about U.S. plans. V-mail solved both problems. Letters written on special sheets were **censored**, photographed, shrunk, and stored on special film. When V-mail letters arrived at their destinations, they were enlarged and printed.

Keeping Up on the Home Front

On the home front, American civilians, factories, and businesses supported the U.S. Army by working to keep the soldiers supplied. Often, teenagers worked. Women worked in factories and in nursing. Some joined the Red Cross, an international organization that helps people in need at wartime. Other women worked in shipyards or on railroads.

Women like this welder entered jobs they had rarely been allowed to take before.

There was not enough food or other supplies to support both the military and the people at home. In 1942, everything from gasoline, rubber, and nylon to sugar, butter, and meat became rationed in the United States. People used government coupons to buy goods. When they had used all of their coupons, they could not buy more of those goods. No new cars were made until 1945. Factories instead made tanks, airplanes, and bombs.

A young girl hands food stamps to the clerk at a grocery store.

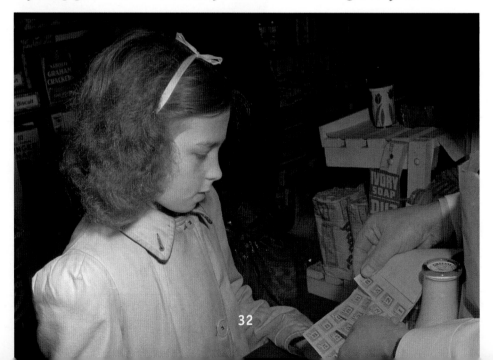

The Holocaust

The war was worst for groups targeted by the Nazis. The main target was the Jewish people. Roma, disabled people, Communists, homosexuals, and other groups also suffered. These people were held in **concentration camps**. Most died of abuse or starvation, or were killed in mass murders. An estimated 6 million Jewish people and millions more from other groups died before Allied soldiers freed the prisoners. This event became known as the Holocaust. The name comes from a Greek word for a burnt religious sacrifice.

U.S. soldiers working at a supply depot in England take a break together for a meal.

CHAPTER 4

Challenges and Changes

During World War II, the vast majority of people in the U.S. Army were white and male. From the beginning, people who were not white were given few opportunities to serve. There were limits on women, too. Even when they were accepted into the army, non-whites and women were put into segregated units. Often, their roles were limited to service jobs. However, as the war progressed, the need for troops grew, so restrictions changed.

← The U.S. military did not adopt a policy of equal rights until 1946.

A Chance to Fight

At the beginning of the war, most African Americans were not allowed in combat. Usually, they transported supplies or built roads. Some served as part of the Red Ball Express, a supply truck convoy. These men brought about half a million tons of supplies to the Allied troops that were pushing the German army out of France.

As the war continued, black soldiers were given more opportunities to become infantrymen, pilots, medics, and officers.

An army officer waves on a supply truck driving along the Red Ball Highway.

From left to right, pilots Benjamin Davis and Edward Gleed stand by one of their planes.

The 332nd Fighter Group was nicknamed the Red Tails, for the red-painted tails on their planes.

The United States' first black fighter pilots were trained in Tuskegee, Alabama. Starting in 1943, these pilots often escorted bombers in and around Italy as the 332nd Fighter Group. They were so effective that many bomber pilots requested them specifically. Farther north, a black tanker unit helped capture 30 major cities in France, Belgium, and Germany. Some African Americans volunteered as riflemen to support white units. They helped win important battles across Europe.

Japanese Americans arrive at a relocation center in California.

Remembering Pearl Harbor

Japan attacked the U.S. naval base at Pearl Harbor, Hawaii, on December 7, 1941. Afterward, many white Americans didn't trust Japanese Americans. In 1942, Japanese Americans stopped being drafted. Most who were already serving in the military were kicked out of it. More than 100,000 Japanese Americans living on the West Coast of the United States were sent to special "wartime communities." These were internment camps with harsh living conditions. They were surrounded by barbed wire fences and guarded by the army.

Many Japanese Americans still wanted to serve their country. Some volunteered as spies and **translators** for U.S. forces in the Pacific. Then, in 1942, the Japanese American 100th Infantry Battalion was created. It later became part of the larger Japanese American 442nd Regimental Combat Team. The team became one of the most decorated U.S. Army units in World War II.

The 100th Infantry Battalion's motto was Remember Pearl Harbor.

39

Women at War

Women worked in the army for the first time in U.S. history during World War II. In previous wars, women had worked as nurses. Starting in 1942, the Women's Army **Auxiliary** Corps (WAAC) gave them more opportunities. In 1943, the unit was granted more importance and renamed the Women's Army Corps (WAC). WACs were not allowed in combat. Instead, each WAC was intended to "free a man for combat" by taking over a noncombat job.

A group of WACs stand at Right Dress (looking to the right) during training.

The first African American WACs were sent overseas in February 1945.

Many WACs worked as secretaries. Some operated radios. WACs also worked in the medical corps. A few women were electricians or mechanics. Others directed airplane traffic or forecasted the weather.

A separate group of women worked with the air force. The organization was called the Women Airforce Service Pilots (WASP). Though WASPs flew military planes, they were civilian volunteers. WACs were official members of the U.S. Army. WASPs were not.

Objecting to War

Some people were against the violence of war and refused to fight during World War II. These people often refused for religious, political, or ethical reasons. They were given a choice: serve in the medical corps, or work at home to support the war. Some worked in hospitals or as firefighters. Others helped grow crops. A small number refused all these choices and went to jail. People who stayed home often lost their jobs or were called cowards.

Timeline of the U.S. Army During World War II

1940
The U.S. government begins drafting men into the army.

1941
The United States enters the war.

The War's End

The war ended in 1945. Germany surrendered on May 7, and Japan surrendered in August. During the war, more than 1 million Americans were killed or wounded. Roughly 900,000 of them were members of the army. After the war, those who survived went to college or returned to work. Many married and started families. Having lived through the bloodiest conflict in world history, they did their best to adjust to living at home and in peace. ★

1942
Rationing begins in the United States to provide supplies to the army and other military branches; the Women's Army Auxiliary Corps is created.

1943
Tuskegee-trained fighter pilots see their first combat; the 100th Infantry Battalion arrives in Europe.

1945
World War II ends.

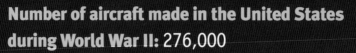

True Statistics

Number of aircraft made in the United States during World War II: 276,000

Number of people in the U.S. Army in 1939: Less than 200,000

Number of people in the U.S. Army in 1945: More than 8 million

Number of U.S. troops involved in the first day of the 1944 invasion of Normandy, France: 73,000

Weight of the gear carried by the average U.S. infantryman: About 60 lb. (27 kg)

Percentage of all U.S. Army casualties who fought as ground forces: About 80

The longest length of time spent in combat by a single U.S. infantry unit: 654 days

Did you find the truth?

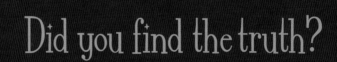

F Some women fought in combat units for the U.S. Army during World War II.

T Civilian groups in Germany worked to overthrow the country's Nazi government.

Resources

Books

Callery, Sean. *World War II*. New York: Scholastic, 2013.

Lessman, Steve. *D-Day: American Character*. Stillwater, OK: New Forums Press, 2010.

Samuels, Charlie. *Soldiers*. Tucson, AZ: Brown Bear Books, 2011.

Visit this Scholastic Web site for more information on the U.S. Army in World War II:

www.factsfornow.scholastic.com

Enter the keywords **U.S. Army in World War II**

Important Words

ammunition (am-yuh-NISH-uhn) — things such as bullets or shells that can be fired from weapons

auxiliary (ahg-ZIL-yur-ee) — available to provide extra help when it is needed

censored (SEN-surd) — changed to remove parts that are thought to be dangerous or unacceptable

civilians (suh-VIL-yuhnz) — people who are not members of the armed forces

concentration camps (kahn-sen-TRAY-shuhn KAMPS) — prisons where large numbers of people who are not soldiers are kept during a war and are usually forced to live in very bad conditions

corps (KOR) — a company of military officers and enlisted people

draft (DRAFT) — to require young men to serve in the armed forces

Nazi (NAHT-see) — member of the political group that ruled Germany from 1933 to 1945

rations (RASH-uhnz) — limited amounts or shares, especially of food

resistance (ri-ZIS-tuhns) — the act of resisting or fighting back

translators (TRANZ-lay-turz) — people who change spoken or written words from one language to another

Index

Page numbers in **bold** indicate illustrations

About the Author

Peter Benoit is the author of dozens of books for Children's Press. He has written about American history, ancient civilizations, ecosystems, and more. Peter is also a historical reenactor, occasional tutor, and poet. He is a graduate of Skidmore College, with a degree in mathematics. He lives in Greenwich, New York.